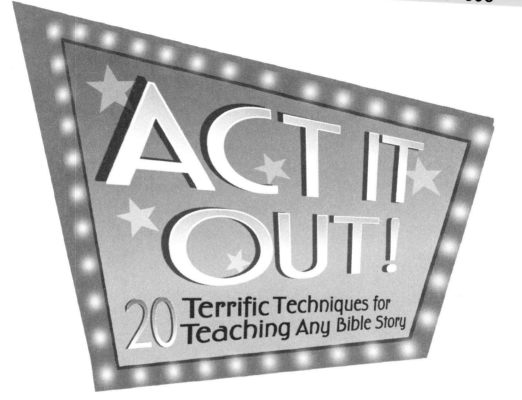

ACT IT OUT!

20 Terrific Techniques for Teaching Any Bible Story

RANDY L. RITZ

STANDARD PUBLISHING

Cincinnati, Ohio

The Standard Publishing Company, Cincinnati, Ohio
A division of Standex International Corporation
© 1999 by The Standard Publishing Company
Printed in the United States of America
All rights reserved

06 05 04 03 02 01 00 99   5 4 3 2 1

Designed and illustrated by Liz Howe
Edited by Lise Caldwell

Ritz, Randy.
   Act it out! : 20 terrific techniques for teaching any Bible story
/ Randy Ritz.
      p.   cm.
   ISBN 0-7847-0919-X
   1. Drama in Christian education.   2. Bible—Study and teaching.
 I. Title.
BV1534.4.R58   1999
268 ' .67—dc21

Table of Contents

Introduction

For those of you brave enough to read this introductory section—here are two brief ideas that Christian educators and youth leaders should know about.

1. Drama as a learning strategy will be one of the key elements in Christian education in the future. The "active learning" component of drama meets a number of classroom needs:

☆ Drama helps students remember the lesson.

☆ Drama provides educational entertainment.

☆ Drama extends the attention spans of students while improving concentration.

☆ Drama provides help for students (and teachers) caught in the attention deficit disorder (ADD) and attention deficit disorder with hyperactivity (ADHD) avalanche.

Although drama is a relatively new strategy for learning, it can continually adjust and evolve with the needs of any classroom and the preferences of any teacher. Drama will not be a fad.

2. Drama will be one of the key methods of evangelism in the future. Churches are searching for ways to involve youth (and adults, for that matter) in evangelism. Yet providing a simple and articulate way of organizing outreach teams has been difficult for many church leaders. With drama's ability to involve many participants at once and its communication and storytelling strength, drama meets a number of evangelism needs:

☆ Drama provides a wonderful framework for young people to present the message of the Gospel.

☆ Drama can present a meaningful and emotional message.

☆ Students feel safe with drama because it is a group effort.
☆ Students experience what it means to be of service to others.

The step from active learning to performance evangelism is a small one. Many of the dramas in this book can easily be adjusted for performance situations. Students actively learn as they create the dramatic sketches, and the learning continues as students present or perform their work for others. There are more suggestions about performance at the back of the book.

What Will This Book Do For You?

Above all, this book will fit easily into any of the stories already being used in a curriculum. To add a drama to a lesson takes only minutes once a teacher understands a particular technique.

This book presents simple strategies for transforming learning into an active experience in children's ministry.

This book will demonstrate the simple techniques and control devices that master drama teachers use successfully.

This is a book for teachers and group leaders on how to use drama, without scripts and memorization, in any classroom.

It will show how drama can be done in any space, including small Sunday school classrooms.

Many of these dramas can be performed for others in a public, educational, or church setting.

This is a learning method that can translate rote knowledge (the facts) into personal experience.

PART I

Act It Out in the Classroom: What Is Drama-Active Learning and Why Should Teachers Use It?

Drama

Drama is essentially about struggle. A struggle can be small: a worker borrows an ax and then the ax head falls into the water, then he is confronted by the owner of the ax. A struggle can be monumental: Abraham prepares to sacrifice his son. A dramatic situation comes from the way that a person struggles to get out of the problem that he is in. The Bible is full of dramatic situations such as these:

☆ As Samson's hair grows again, will he regain his strength and be able to judge his enemies?

☆ Will Abraham be able to save anyone in the city before Sodom is destroyed by fire?

☆ How will Zacchaeus manage to see and meet Jesus?

☆ How will Mary trust Jesus again when he let her brother Lazarus die?

Dramatic situations are so appealing because adults, youth, and children can all identify emotionally with the person's struggle to get out of the problem. Creating a drama happens when students (of any age) are allowed to act out or "become" the character who is struggling—they enter into the dramatic situation and learn by sharing the character's victories, defeats, joys, struggles, and even pain.

What Is Active Learning?

There appears to be a great deal of confusion in educational circles as to what "active learning" is. My view is quite simple. In the past, educators have made the retention and memorization of facts the utmost goal of learning. This is frequently called "banking learning" where the mind (and its functions of memory and thought) are privileged or prioritized over the emotions, expression, and movement of the body. If students can recite a memorized verse or regurgitate information on a test form, then they are deemed to have "learned" it. That is the intent of "banking learning." A teacher might think, "If we can just get the student to remember the facts and information, when the need arises, the student can draw on that bank of knowledge and use it." The assumption is that if we have *memorized* information, we also *understand* it. I think not.

I do believe in laying a foundation of knowledge and presenting hard facts to students, but I like to wrap these facts in a dramatic context, not just a cognitive/verbal one. Imagine that drama-active learning is a skeleton. The emotional, expressive, and personal experience of drama-active learning is the framework to which the tendons, muscle, and flesh of hard facts are attached. The memorization of facts is easier (and makes sense) because the facts are associated with an experience.

If you have been around education for a while you may have encountered this statement attributed to Confucius: "I hear, I forget. I see, I remember. I do, I understand." The "doing" is really the heart of drama-active learning because it leads to understanding. If teachers tell their students something—even if the students can restate it—there is a good chance that they will forget. If teachers take the next step and demonstrate through acting out or illustrating the facts, the students may remember the information. But when the students themselves approach the information via drama-active learning (or any form of active learning), and are led to reflect on the lessons inherent in the active experience, they begin to understand.

Ownership

Teachers can create a teaching event or dramatic activity that will give students the room and opportunity to make the knowledge their own. For instance, when students act out some part of a story, then they have invested something of themselves into understanding and learning the story. In this way students can "own" the story and the knowledge it reveals. The teacher then must draw out the facts and the feelings from the students. This is done by asking good questions and making factual connections for the students.

What Kinds of Events Am I Suggesting?

Have students become reporters, write a poem about the feeling surrounding the story, create a collage, paint a painting, mold clay, hold a debate that gives opportunity for students to examine other sides of an issue, or do a radio play about a biblical event. Let students tell a story backed by mood music. Let students perform for younger grades, and of course, have them do a drama!

Drama-Active Learning

Drama-active learning is an exciting way of taking a Bible story and making an event out of it—an experiential activity in which students get into the action and become some or all of the Bible characters in the story. You, as teacher, put this drama-active learning into your lesson plan by choosing one of the 20 drama activities in this book and applying it to any story or theme found in your curriculum.

A terrific example is the story of the disciples huddling in fear of the storm, while Jesus sleeps in the boat (Luke 8:22-25). The students assume the characters of the disciples. In this drama-active event the students/disciples could:

- ☆ fish, hoist the sails, or be seasick before the storm hits
- ☆ decide if they will wake up Jesus
- ☆ elect a leader to wake Jesus up
- ☆ create a storm with sound effects
- ☆ become the storming seas by using cloth or movement
- ☆ try to bail the boat
- ☆ take down the sails
- ☆ be fearful of the power of Jesus (when he calms the storm)
- ☆ bow down and worship Jesus

The possibilities for action in this story are numerous, but what will the students gain from this experience? Students identify with and pull from the dramatic event unique and personal insights. But because each student is different, with different learning styles and different interests, some students will make emotional discoveries ("I've been fearful like the disciples."); some will stretch physically ("I never thought I could create a storm with just my voice."). Others will push or expand their "comfort zones" ("I was a bit scared when I had to stand on a chair and shout, 'Peace, be still.'"), and others will learn facts ("My group made frozen pictures of the beginning, middle, and the end—I know the whole story.").

It is important to draw these discoveries out of the students and help them make sense of their "just completed" experience. Following the drama-active event, the teacher or leader needs to ask good questions. Some sample questions could be:

- ☆ What part of this drama most excited you?
- ☆ When has God gotten you out of a scary situation?

☆ Would it be easier to believe in God (or Jesus) if you had been on that boat with the disciples?

☆ What was the last thing the disciples did in this story? What does it mean to worship Jesus?

These questions (and others) should start a great discussion which can focus the class on the goals of the lesson. After some discussion, the teacher will move on to the rest of the prepared lesson found in the curriculum. I believe that good questions are essential to drama-active learning. That is why I have included questions in each of the twenty drama activities.

When you look at the next section, "How to Prepare for Drama and Keep It Under Control," take a look at how information and understanding can be drawn from the experience of students participating in a drama.

PART 2

How to Prepare for Drama and Keep It Under Control

It would be wonderful if a leader could simply set up a drama and let it run. However, this is not the case. Drama takes constant tinkering. Drama-active learning is not difficult, but adjustments are necessary due to the complexity of human nature. Each student will have had a different family environment and upbringing. This will affect the behavior and communication between students. Each student will come to class in a different emotional state, with various fears and expectations. This will affect the group's focus and the students' ability to be vulnerable. On occasion you, as teacher, may not feel energetic or confident, and so your normal leadership skills aren't as apparent.

For all of these reasons, and many more, it is important to structure your drama in such a way that it has the best chance for success. In other words, properly planned, the dramatic experience will happen, even if the emotional and physical states of the students or leaders are subpar.

In this section I want to provide step-by-step instructions on how to plan a drama, how to set up a classroom for drama, how to control students who will not be sitting in chairs (and who will make some noise!), and how to use time as a control device and as a way to motivate students.

Four Steps to Plan a Drama

Once you have tried these four steps a few times, the step-by-step process becomes second nature. It becomes easier for you to decide which part of the lesson to dramatize. Preparation takes less time as you quickly identify what the specific needs of each drama are (whether it's a tape deck or five photocopies of the same story). You will find it easier to ask good questions. The four steps are:

Step 1. Select a Bible story. (Each activity in this book includes possible "Stories and Themes" and "Learner Goals.")

Step 2. Select an activity from the book. (Each activity includes "At-a-Glance," a step-by-step description of how to lead the drama activity.)

Step 3. Prepare the drama activity. (Each drama activity includes "Preparation" suggestions.)

Step 4. Ask questions about the drama experience. (Each drama activity includes "Questions.")

Step 1: Selecting a Story

Look under "Themes and Stories" in each of the twenty drama activities. The suggested Christian themes and biblical stories provided work well with that specific drama, but are not exhaustive. Under "Learner Goals" you will find basic, yet important outcomes, benefits, or objectives for each drama. To begin, identify a story or parts of a story. The story can come from many sources, such as a Sunday school or Christian education curriculum lesson, a specific Bible story that interests you, a poem, a modern situation or newspaper article, or a short story with a spiritual theme. Be creative. If you brainstorm, you will discover many stories that can be adapted to a lesson.

Step 2: Selecting a Drama Activity

To help you understand the structure of the drama activities and break each one down into a timed, step-by-step synopsis, the "At-a-Glance" section is provided. These simple instructions include suggested time limits for each portion of the drama. As you read through and experiment with each drama, it becomes easier to identify which will work best with what story, theme, or character.

Choose the drama that will bring the selected story alive or will help the students experience the theme for the lesson. If the key to the lesson is a Bible character, then choose one of the "Character Dramas." If the story is important and you want students to get the facts then a "Story Drama," which outlines the beginning, middle, and end of the story, would be suitable. If a concept, such as forgiveness, or theme, such as "love your neighbor," is to be taught, then choose one of the "Theme Dramas."

Step 3: Prepare the Drama Activity

The drama activity will go more smoothly if you plan ahead. Look in the "Preparation" section to ensure a successful experience for yourself and your students. Do you need boundaries for the students if there is movement? What control devices will you use to stop the students once you get them going? Do you need any taped music? Do you have enough Bibles in case the students don't bring their own? Are there any special room or activity needs?

Step 4: Ask Questions About the Drama Experience

In each activity you will find a "Questions" section with a list of questions that relate to that specific drama experience. Usually, however, you will need to determine what questions will lead your students to reflection and discussion. Avoid asking rhetorical or one-word answer questions such as "Do you think the disciples were afraid?" The only answer to this question is "yes" or "no." Students tire of this type of questions very quickly. Instead, ask open-ended and thought-provoking questions. The following questions could be asked about the story of the Lord passing over the homes of the children of Israel in Egypt (Exodus 12). Notice the use of the senses.

☆ What would it have been like to be a child that day?

☆ What would the weather have been like? Do you think that everyone in the houses slept that night? Why or why not?

☆ What do you think the family discussed at supper?

☆ What was Moses thinking about that night?

What Happens Next?

Each drama includes a section called "Key Points," which includes warnings about potential trouble spots and emphasizes crucial points that must be addressed. The next section, "Extensions," is an idea bank that suggests ways to change a drama if a you wish to repeat or expand it. Sometimes these suggestions make a drama progressively more challenging; other times an extension identifies ways to make a drama more polished and performable. Remember, no matter what happens in your drama, make sure students understand what really happened in the Bible.

Using Other Stories

I find that many children's storybooks have spiritual themes. For elementary students I might suggest stories such as "The Fox and the Crow" *(Aesop's Fables),* which explores vanity; *Where the Wild Things Are*, by Maurice Sendak, which explores creation and creativity; *The Selfish Giant*, by Oscar Wilde, which explores God's ability to change the heart of humankind; and *Love You Forever*, by Robert Munsch, which focuses on commitment and unconditional love. I am sure that you will have favorites as well.

If the class is composed of older students, then the teacher has the challenge of finding books with a more mature approach.

Secular children's stories, however, can still be part of a junior or senior high school class when the intent is to lead youth in hands-on ministry or service. The older students can perform these simple stories for audiences comprised of elementary students. As the youth interact with the children, they minister to them.

Why would you want to use such books? It is my belief that one of the biggest challenges in Christian education is the boredom factor. Students, with good intentions and good hearts, can grow weary of hearing the same Bible stories over and over again. This book is, in part, a response to the boredom factor. If teachers can find new, experiential ways of looking at fundamental stories, then the learning process is rejuvenated. Another way to refresh the learning process in Sunday school rooms is to add literature which supports biblical themes. Teachers need to use God's wisdom in choosing non-biblical stories and deciding what will enhance the classroom experience for their students.

Classroom Set-Up

Classrooms are not sacred—move the tables, chairs, or desks around in any way which makes more room for drama. Christian educators everywhere are struggling with small classroom space. Don't let this stop you from trying drama-active learning! Time spent on moving furniture is not wasted if you believe that students learn by doing as well as hearing. Just make sure your students know where everything should go.

Train your class to move desks, tables, and chairs out of the way quickly. Decide, before you give any instructions, where each furniture item will be moved and which students will be assigned to move which object. After a drama activity, the students can sit on the floor to continue the class (particularly to discuss). Moving things out of the way takes practice but eventually your group will become more efficient at it.

Controlling Your Students

My firm belief is that you cannot really teach anything or lead a group of energetic students in drama unless there is first and foremost control. You need not be harsh or punitive in the way you control your students. Give students clear boundaries as to what they can or cannot do. Tell them when they should stop and listen, and then maintain that boundary with gentle firmness. Don't go on with any discussion or exercise until each student is following instructions.

If adult or youth helpers are in the class, make sure that these leaders participate in the drama. The reason behind this is simple—adult role models who join in with enthusiasm will help students overcome reluctance to participate. I encourage all students to join in the dramas. Children with learning disabilities or physical disabilities can always find roles as well, and they love it.

Teachers can anticipate problems in the classroom when they are mobile. As the students are doing the drama activity, a roving teacher can find groups who may be "stuck." If one or more groups is having trouble coming up with ideas, they will be kept on task with a kick-start idea from the teacher.

Try a control device which will clearly signal or get the students' attention. This signal will tell them that it is time to begin an activity, time to end an activity, or time to listen to you for more instructions. Some things which work well are ringing a bell, turning the lights off and on, or firmly and sometimes loudly saying "Freeze!" "Freeze!" means students will come to a complete stop with no speaking and no movement. Do not settle for less and do not begin again until everyone has frozen. If done with confidence, high school students will also listen to this command.

As the class does more and more drama work, they will catch on to the "rules" for doing drama, and most of the students will respond to instructions, because the drama is fun.

Controlling Your Time

One of the best motivational and control devices is time limitations. If I allow ten minutes for a group to develop a short dramatic picture or to come up with an idea for a drama, they will take ten minutes. If I give them one minute, they will take only one minute. The rule is that students will use as much time as you give them. Therefore, I give students only the amount of time necessary to complete the task and no more. When using drama in the youth group or classroom we are not aiming for perfection; we are aiming for participation. We are not aiming for art; we are aiming for creativity.

When I tell a class that they will have forty seconds to make a frozen picture of some part of a story, inevitably the work ethic goes way up. There is no time to fool around or to distract others. The concentration and focused energy necessary to complete the task on time demands the full attention of the students. As leader, I move around the room and watch so that I can extend the time if a group looks like they are struggling. I allow one minute for a two-person drama to unfold and let them know when it is about to end. This gently pressures the students to get on-task and not waste time. In the next section you can see how time is assigned for each part of the exercise. Don't be afraid to use a stopwatch.

PART 3

Story Dramas

The following six drama activities provide a variety of ways to tell Bible stories. Students define the beginning, the middle, and the end of a story. In restating the story through drama, students analyze and select what they think is important to the action of the story. This encourages student ownership of the learning process. Students are not just passive recipients of knowledge; they actively engage with the story in question. As they act out the story, the students remember it and begin to understand its significance and its place in the Bible.

For a "Story Drama" to be successful, students need to identify the beginning, the middle, and the end of a story. Limit the middle section of the story to no more than two points of action so that the drama does not get complicated. When working with junior and senior high school students, a teacher can leave these structural decisions to the group. They are able to decide what part of the story should be the beginning, which key moments make up the middle section, and how to end it. If the class or group is younger, the teacher should quickly preview the story and identify the beginning, the middle section, and the end. Underline the four key parts of the story, and then number them.

There are several ways to provide the beginning, middle, and ending points for your acting groups. I provide a Bible for every group. Within this Bible I identify the beginning, the two middle action moments, and the end of the story. Or I photocopy the story and then underline the selected verses or lines. Sometimes I write the four verses on an index card and then hand one card to each group. It is wise to take back the cards after the drama so that they can be used again.

You will find that the following "Story Dramas" will bring to life the stories of the Bible for you and your students in a way you may not have previously imagined.

Sound Effect Story

Themes and Stories

This active drama is a wonderful "first-step" acting experience. It is a great drama to begin with because the students get to perform their final product in front of an audience that will have its eyes closed. "Sound Effect Story" is a drama which uses created sound effects to tell the main parts of a Bible story. Environmental stories, rich in sensory descriptions, work best because they give the students lots of sounds to work with, such as wind, animals, rain, cheering, and music. To get the class going, a warm-up activity—an introduction to this kind of drama—might be helpful. A great story for the first time through this activity is the story of Gideon from Judges 7, which provides ample opportunity for sound effects.

Consider using these Bible stories:
The Creation (Genesis 1)
The Flood (Genesis 7)
Jacob's Dream (Genesis 28:10-17)
The Parting of the Red Sea (Exodus 14)
The Lord Appears to Elijah (1 Kings 19:9-18)
The Second Coming (Luke 21:10-28)

Learner Goals

"Sound Effect Story" helps students
☆ explore their voices,
☆ restate a familiar story,
☆ gain confidence in performing,
☆ cooperate with one another.

Preparation

Make sure that you have enough stories so that you can assign one story to each group (the groups can be made up of ten students or fewer). Each group should have either a Bible (with the reference for the story), a photocopy of the story, or a card identifying the key parts of the story.

Identify the action of the story by underlining, numbering, or writing out one beginning verse, two middle verses, and a final verse.

Sound Effect Story

 1 Divide your class into groups of ten students or fewer. Have each group sit in a circle (one minute).

2 Give a different story to each group. The beginning, middle, and end of each story should be clearly marked and numbered. The group chooses a narrator who reads the assigned story out loud to those in his group, and who will later read when the story is performed for the class (three minutes).

 3 The groups rehearse the story by adding sound effects. As the narrator speaks each of the four narration verses, each group recreates the action using only sound effects for each verse. Vocal noises and physical noises (chairs tipping, paper ripping, etc.) can be used. More than one person can make the same sound; for example, five people can be Goliath (ten minutes).

 4 The class sits to hear each of the groups perform its "Sound Effect Story," but the members of the class/audience must have their eyes closed (two minutes times the number of groups performing).

5 Follow each performance with a lively discussion using the questions that follow and others you create.

Questions

○ From this group's presentation, what sounds did you like best?
○ When you were performing, how did having everyone else's eyes closed affect your performance?
○ How was God faithful to this Bible character?
○ If you were one of the people in this story, what would you have done?

Key Points

☆ Keep groups on task and on time. If you give students excess time they will waste it. Use a stop watch.
☆ The class/audience can huddle in the middle of the room so that the performing group can move all around them. This adds to the movement and effect of the sound.

Extension

Groups could choose to use the complete stories as the narration rather than just four lines. Because of the added words, students would need to give more thought to where the specific sound effects can be inserted into each story. The "Sound Effect Story" then becomes like a radio play performed live. Because of the extra work and extra rehearsal (perhaps), these stories can be presented in front of an "eyes open" audience. This works particularly well with junior and senior high school students.

Music Story

Themes and Stories

This is my all-time favorite drama activity because it draws on the students' love of catchy energetic music and, more importantly for leaders, because it is a nonverbal drama that can be controlled easily. "Music Story" can be used with any action-based story. The success of this drama rests on finding a short piece or portion of music which has the emotional atmosphere that you want. The music could have a mechanical tempo, a mysterious dark chord structure, an adventuresome and carefree melody, a military rhythm section, a soothing arrangement, a light comical feel, or glorious strings. Look for movie themes, musical interludes in songs, classical music, and meditative music as sources from which stories can be built upon. Keep the music length around 2.5 minutes or less. Some music selections that I frequently use are "In the Hall of the Mountain King," *Peer Gynt*, Edvard Grieg; "Sabre Dance," *Gayane*, Aram Khatchaturian; and the *Fantasia* soundtrack, various selections.

The following Bible stories have action and emotional atmosphere:
Joshua Marching Around Jericho (Joshua 6:1-21)
Gideon Fighting the Midianites (Judges 6:36–7:21)
Daniel in the Den of Lions (Daniel 6:1-23)
The Resurrection of Christ (Luke 24:1-12)

Learner Goals

"Music Story" helps students
☆ tell stories in different ways,
☆ work with rhythm and tempo,
☆ push their creative boundaries,
☆ break down shyness and get everyone involved.

Preparation

Select an emotionally dynamic piece of music, approximately two minutes in length. The music should have some kind of tempo change during the two minute playing time and should fit with the action of the story. In order to find two minutes of music, begin and end the piece when you want it to (just fade it out or in). Remember to bring a tape or CD player, and know the general plot of the story (or stories) you want your group to act out.

Music Story

 Make groups of any size and have them all listen to the same two-minute piece of music. The music should bring to mind several Bible stories, one of which the group can choose. Or you can provide a story which fits with the music (two minutes).

 Play the music a second time while the groups begin to act out the story—using only actions, not words (three minutes).

 Play the music two more times as groups act and rehearse their story. Between the times you play the song, include some non-music work time and discussion time (six minutes).

 Have each group performs its "Music Story" piece for the other groups (two minutes times the number of groups performing).

 Follow each performance with lively discussion based on the questions that follow and others you create.

Questions

○ What part of the group's presentation did you like best?
○ How did you feel performing your story for the rest of the class?
○ Why did God allow this problem or event to happen?
○ What is God saying to us today by putting the story in the Bible?

Key Points

☆ "Music Story" can be performed by large groups as well as small groups. The whole class can do one story.
☆ Make sure that the groups get onto their feet and move when you play the music for the second time.
☆ Keep a tight rein on the discussion time between each time the music is played.
☆ Carefully watch the groups to determine if there is a need to play the music one more time.

Frozen Pictures

Themes and Stories

This drama presents the quickest way of finding the action moments in any story (remember the beginning, two middles, and an end). It is also the quickest way of getting students to "become" a Bible character. A "Frozen Picture" is a group statue or "snapshot" of one dramatic moment in a story. Just like a photograph, the picture is more interesting when action is present. The frozen picture needs to capture the highest activity level possible. A frozen picture of someone holding a baseball bat may be somewhat interesting, but if you can capture the actual moment the bat connects for a home run, then you have made a great frozen picture.

These Bible stories work well with "Frozen Pictures:"
The Golden Calf (Exodus 32:19)
Elijah and the Prophets of Baal (1 Kings 18:16-40)
The Fiery Furnace (Daniel 3:8-30)
The Wedding Banquet (Matthew 22:1-14)
Saul's Conversion (Acts 9:1-19)

Learner Goals

"Frozen Pictures" helps students

☆ quickly identify the beginning, middle, and end of a Bible story,

☆ learn while being very active,

☆ break down "cliques" because gifted and non-gifted students (intellectually, theatrically, verbally) work together easily in this project.

Preparation

Make sure that you have enough stories so that you can assign one story to each group (the groups can be composed of ten or fewer). Six students per group is the best ratio for this project. Each group should have either a Bible (with the reference for the story), a photocopy of the story, or a card identifying the key parts of the story.

Identify the beginning, middle, and ending by underlining, numbering, or writing out one beginning verse, two middle verses, and an ending verse.

Frozen Pictures

 Divide your class into groups composed of equal numbers (six per group is best) and have each group sit in a circle (one minute).

 Give the same story (or a different story depending on your goals) to each group. The action verses should be clearly marked and numbered. The group chooses a narrator who reads the assigned story out loud to those in her group (three minutes).

 At the command to "Begin," all groups work simultaneously in making a frozen picture of their first action verse. Use the command "Freeze!" after one minute to help groups hold the frozen picture (one minute).

 Once Frozen Picture number one is complete, then repeat the process to make Frozen Pictures for the two middle action verses and the end line. Give only one minute to create each frozen picture and don't forget to say, "Freeze!" (three minutes).

 Groups perform or show their Frozen Pictures to the rest of the class. Each group can read the four verses when presenting if they wish (two minutes times the number of groups performing).

 Follow each performance with lively discussion based on the questions that follow and others you create.

Questions

○ What was one interesting moment in the pictures you saw in the group?
○ What was the problem in this story?
○ What did you learn about this story as you made these pictures?
○ In what ways was God involved in this story?

Key Points

☆ Student actors can become walls, trees, extra guards, animals, etc. This becomes important when there are more people in each group than there are characters in the story. Encourage creativity and humor.

☆ Once the four Frozen Pictures are completed, I suggest that the teacher quickly run through all four pictures again to solidify the "snapshots" in the minds of the student actors.

☆ Keep the one minute time boundaries for each Frozen Picture. This keeps each group focused and on task.

Extension

See Story Drama 4: Moving Pictures

Moving Pictures

Themes and Stories

This is a natural extension from Story Drama 3: Frozen Pictures. The idea is to take four "Frozen Pictures" and then bring them to life with words, sounds, and actions. This drama works well with just about any story. If the story selected has only a few persons (for example only Paul, Silas, and the jailer) and each group has six or seven students, you as teacher need to be creative. Suggest that the non-speaking students in each group use their imagination and become trees, guards, the wind, sun, walls, animals, angels, water, and the like. As this drama will "come to life," the sounds that accompany the water, wind, or animals will do much to enhance the drama and may provide some comedy as well.

Once each of the four "Frozen Pictures" have come to life and the students have created their own dialogue, the class is well on the way to creating its own play—a play that is based on a "no memorization" concept.

Consider these Bible stories:
Wise and Foolish Builders (Matthew 7:24-27)
Parable of the Sower (Matthew 13:3-9)
Parable of the Unmerciful Servant (Matthew 18:23-35)
Paul and Silas in Prison (Acts 16:20-31)
any of the stories from "Frozen Pictures"

Learner Goals

"Moving Pictures" help students
☆ reflect on the key meaning of a Bible story,
☆ work as a group,
☆ initiate creative problem solving,
☆ improve verbal and non-verbal communication skills.

Preparation

Skim "Frozen Pictures" so you will know the foundation of this exercise. Make sure that you have enough stories so that you can assign one story to each group (the groups can be made up of ten or fewer). Six students per group is the best for this project.

Each group should have either a Bible (with the reference for the story), a photocopy of the story, or a card identifying the key parts of the story. Identify the beginning, two middle, and ending action verses by underlining, numbering, or writing out one beginning verse, two middle verses, and an end verse.

Moving Pictures

 Have groups form four Frozen Pictures of a story (see Frozen Pictures to find out how to get to this point) (four minutes).

 Give instructions: "Make the Frozen Picture number one and don't move. When I say 'Go,' again I want groups to come to life for ten seconds and make the noise or say the words you think the people in this story would say." Give the command "Go!" and after ten seconds say, "Freeze!" (forty-five seconds).

 Say to the students, "Make the Frozen Picture number two and freeze in the picture. When I say, 'Go!' you will come to life for ten seconds." Give the command "Go!" and after ten seconds say, "Freeze!" Do Pictures three and four the same way (thirty seconds times remaining Frozen Pictures).

 Groups perform individual stories for the class/audience. Teacher will have to call, "Go!" and "Freeze!" for each group (two minutes times the number of groups performing).

 Follow each performance with lively discussion based on the questions that follow and others you create.

Questions

○ Do you think all of the words found in the Bible were actually spoken? How can we know?
○ What was your favorite part of the performance?
○ Why did God put this particular story in the Bible?

Key Points

☆ Make sure each group has made the Frozen Picture before they come to life.
☆ Call "Freeze," after ten seconds of dialogue and sound.

Extension

Ask each group to take ten minutes and smooth out any of the dialogue problems they might have. In other words, have them make it better. Ask the students to also include a narrator from the group (one who will read the verses associated with the four "Frozen Pictures").

Each group must also decide when they will begin each Moving Picture and when they will stop or freeze. What signal will they use to get the whole group to work together?

When this is completed, these dramas are ready to be presented to an audience.

Echo Storytelling

Themes and Stories

The "echo" part of this "Story Drama" consists of the class repeating phrases, sounds, and movements that you, the teacher, make. There is no way around solid preparation for this drama, because you must initiate all of the action in this story. It does, however, come much easier after you have tried it a few times. Tell a Bible story one phrase at a time. At the end of each phrase, add a physical movement (and sound if desired) that relates to the action of the lines spoken. The whole class immediately repeats or "echoes" the words and the actions in unison. The important thing to remember is that you as a leader do not need to tell every moment of the story. It is normal to miss a few bits of the story. This can be corrected; a good follow-up discussion can point out the missing pieces to the story.

This "Story Drama" is good with just about any narrative story.
Be bold and try some unusual ones with this method:
Joseph Meets His Brothers (Genesis 48)
Deborah and Barak (Judges 4:4-23)
Christ Is Born (Luke 2:1-20)
Parable of the Sower and the Seeds (Mark 4:3-20)
Peter Is Released From Prison (Acts 12:1-19)

Learner Goals

"Echo Storytelling" helps students
☆ expand their comfort zones—explore new physical movements,
☆ review or preview stories,
☆ build group spirit and cooperation,
☆ project their voices.

Preparation

Take one large index card and draw a line down the center. On the left side write the main action phrases of your story. On the right side suggest a simple physical action that corresponds with the phrase. You should have between fifteen and twenty phrases and actions.

Practice holding the card in one hand as you tell the story and do the actions. This will help you remember the sequence of the story. It is quite acceptable to forget parts of the story. No one will know about the story line gap but you. Remember, you can fill in the gaps when you have a discussion.

Read the full story and make mental "road map" markers to help you fill in the story surrounding the action phrases written on the card.

Echo Storytelling

 1 Clear tables and chairs for this drama if possible. Have the class stand in a circle so that all students can see you (one and one-half minutes).

 2 Tell the story phrase by phrase. Demonstrate a simple movement (and sound if desired) that fits with the words. For example, if you were telling the story of Paul looking out the prison window, you might make a move to grab the bars and look (five- to ten-second phrases).

 3 Students, in unison, echo the teacher's phrase, including the teacher's movements and sounds, if any (five- to ten-second phrase echo).

 4 Complete the story with actions and sounds throughout (two-minute story).

 5 Follow each performance with lively discussion based on the questions that follow and others you create.

Questions

○ What is the most important part of this story, in your opinion?
○ If you were this biblical character, what, if anything, would you have done differently?
○ What sounds did you like the best?
○ What actions were the most fun for you?

Key Points

☆ Keep the class in a circle so that the students can always see your actions.
☆ Write phrases, not full sentences, on the card.
☆ Encourage students to repeat the phrase and action immediately after you have stopped. Don't give them time to think or become embarrassed.
☆ Keep the phrases and actions well-paced.

Example

Here is an example of the story of Acts 12:1-19.

Teacher: Peter shook off the chains (shakes hands and feet).

Students: Peter shook off the chains (shake hands and feet).

Teacher: He walked slowly to the door as he looked around (looks all around to see if guards are present).

Students: He walked slowly to the door as he looked around (look around to see if guards are present).

Teacher: And Peter opened the door with a creak (teacher mimes opening a door and makes a creaking sound).

Students: And Peter opened the door with a creak (students make a "creeeaak" sound).

Teacher-Led Drama

In this drama, the teacher takes on the role of a biblical leader, and the class becomes the followers. The teacher leads the class in belief-building activities. The teacher and the students need only do the dramatic activities that the story suggests. I find that this drama works best for five- to twelve-year-olds.

The story of Joshua and the spies works well. The teacher, who plays Joshua, speaks to the class as if they were the spies going into Canaan. When "Joshua" asks the spies to pack supplies into a leather bag, the class does so. Joshua can lead them in sneaking through the land, spying on the giants, and cutting down grapes and then carrying them home. These are belief-building activities.

In the above example there is a teacher role, Joshua, and a student role, the spies; a dramatic action, to spy out a new land; and belief-building activities, preparing for the trip, sneaking through the land, spying on the giants, and cutting down grapes. Each drama can be constructed according to the demands of the story.

Here is another possible story:
Scripture Passage: Exodus 14:19-31
Teacher's Role: Pharaoh
Students' Role: Pharaoh's army
Dramatic Action: Challenge army to go through parted waters.
Belief-Building Activities: Put on armor, harness the horses to the chariots, check bow and arrows, and touch the wall of water.

Learner Goals

"Teacher-Led Drama" helps students

☆ bring out the facts of a story in a dramatic way,

☆ see the teacher in a new light—as a fellow actor,

☆ get contextual information (more than just the story) because the teacher can "feed" information to students.

Preparation

Determine the following from the story: the teacher's role, the students' role, and the dramatic action of the story, and list three or four belief-building activities for the students.

Plan to move tables and chairs or find an open area which can be used for ten minutes.

Read the entire story so that information can be fed or presented to the students while they are acting it out.

Teacher-Led Drama

 Read the story to the class. Assume the leadership role (Joshua, for example) and assign the class the role of followers (three minutes).

 Lead the students physically and vocally to prepare for the action to come. Encourage students to sharpen their swords before a battle, collect water for the journey ahead, or put on enemy clothing as a disguise. This builds belief in the drama.

 Lead the class around the room. Coach students to sneak through forests, wade through streams, spy on giants, etc. Return back to camp (or town, or fortress).

 Follow with a lively discussion using the questions that follow and others you create.

Questions

○ In what ways did the characters in this story do the wrong thing?
○ What characters did the right thing? What did they do?
○ What does God promise us if we are obedient?
○ Have you ever had a big challenge? What did you do?

Key Points

☆ "Teacher-Led Drama" can appear to be a risky or challenging strategy. I suggest you just try it. You can always yell, "Freeze," and put the tables back. Take a chance with this—your students will love you for it.

☆ Write down the belief-building activities on an index card that you can hold easily or keep beside you.

☆ The best way to challenge students is to ask them questions. Base the questions on the specific story and on general Bible knowledge (for example, "Is your God strong?" "What did God do for this character?" "What has God done for you?").

Extension

You, the teacher, can play two roles; one as leader of the class and one as enemy of the class. Follow steps 1 through 3 as instructed. Then step away from the rest of the class and change your attitude. Become the enemy leader ready to challenge the students. For example, be Goliath, the captain of an army, or a prophet of Baal. Confront the "enemy" students by questioning them and bragging about the strength of your position. Then return to your role as the students' leader and encourage them to explain why God's power is greater than the enemy's.

PART 4

Character Dramas

"Character Drama" gives students a chance to explore the high and low points of a biblical character. More than that, however, this type of drama opens up the emotional realm of a character by helping students go beneath the facts of the story to the emotional struggle that undergirds it. We all know that Elijah challenged 450 prophets of Baal to bring down fire from heaven. What emotional battle raged within Elijah as he faced the false prophets and the children of Israel? Did he believe fire would fall from above? Did he ever think about what would happen if God failed to answer? It helps young students make sense of their own fears and struggles when they experience, through drama, the fears and struggles of biblical role models and characters.

All of the characters found within these dramas can be played by either male or female actors interchangeably. Although the disciples were all male, it is a simple matter to cast both the male and female students in your class as disciples. When doing a drama, it makes no difference if Peter, when walking on the water, is a man or a woman. Soldiers can also be of either sex. It should be noted, however, that assigning males to play a specifically female part is not always an "easy sell." I have found that when this is tried, the final product is almost always comic because the male will usually exaggerate a female's voice and movements.

"Character Drama" works exceptionally well with partners, making organization and control of the drama more efficient. It does, however, raise the volume of the class at times, so be prepared to occasionally remind students of noise boundaries. Two of my favorite dramas—"Statues" and "Two-Person Drama"—are in this section. They are both easy to plan and execute and richly rewarding as a student experience.

Statues

Themes and Stories

This is one of the easiest dramas to organize and one that invites a lot of laughter. The "potter and clay" motif helps students to mingle and move outside their normal peer groupings. The object of this drama is to shape a partner into a statue of a Bible character. The final picture or shape should show the struggle, or joy, or fear, or power flowing from that character during the moment of crisis.

When the sculptors shape the emotion on the faces and in the bodies of these statues, they learn, as do others who observe, something about the characters themselves. In most cases these Bible characters are like us.

Consider using one of these biblical moments:
The angel guarding the Garden of Eden (Genesis 3)
Lot's wife, as she turns to look at Sodom being destroyed
(Genesis 19:15-26)
Moses, as he raises his staff to part the Red Sea (Exodus 14:10-22)
Mary, as she holds Jesus for the first time (Luke 2:6, 7, 16-19)
Peter, as he walks on water (Matthew 14:22-32)
John, on the Mount of Transfiguration (Luke 9:28-36)

Learner Goals

"Statues" helps students

☆ get involved rather than be indifferent,

☆ discover the hidden emotions surrounding key moments in Bible history,

☆ improve their concentration.

Preparation

Locate specific stories in the Bible that show characters in an emotional or physical struggle, or show them discovering something.

Write a list of six characters on the blackboard. The sculptors may choose one of the six to create a statue of. If you have the time and energy, one character can be given to each student.

Statues

 Divide the class into pairs—one student is the clay and the other is the sculptor (one minute).

 All of the sculptors explore by shaping the arms, legs, body position, and facial expressions of the "human clay" partner. Clay cannot move on its own (two minutes).

 After a twenty-second break sculptors create a "masterpiece" statue of one of the Bible characters in a moment of crisis or discovery (one minute).

 Statues "freeze" and sculptors examine each others' work. Reverse roles and repeat (one minute).

 Follow each performance with lively discussion based on the questions that follow and others you create.

Questions

○ Why did you make your statue in the way you did?
○ What kind of situation (crisis or problem) was your statue in?
○ How would you help your character become a normal or happy person again?

Key Points

✰ After some initial noise, as sculptors and clay get through some nervous laughter, stress that the clay should be silent. This raises the concentration level and keeps the noise level under control.

✰ The clay must keep the shape the sculptor puts him into.
Watch that the clay statues are not in an uncomfortable position for a long period of time (for example, standing on one leg).

✰ Stress absolute silence as the sculptors walk around and look at each other's work. Encourage the clay statues to concentrate hard.

Who Am I?

Themes and Stories

This is one of the simplest acting experiences for elementary students. We often overlook the easiest way to engage our classes. In "Who Am I?" a student acts out a character while the rest of the class tries to identify him or her. The actor, however, cannot use any words. This is a smart way to see what kind of general Bible knowledge a class has.

My expectations are modest with "Who Am I?" I hope that students will be able to identify what is most significant about certain Bible characters. For example, Samson is blinded, placed between two pillars, and destroys the Philistine leadership. As the students see this acted out and discover the identity, I hope that they learn truths about obedience and God's forgiveness. Peter steps out of the boat and after taking a few faltering steps, sinks into the water. Students seeing this may be encouraged to talk about faith and the risks they take in their lives.

Students can also act out these characters:
Adam naming animals (Genesis 2:20)
Job sitting in rags and in pain (Job 2:7)
David fighting a lion (1 Samuel 17:34-37)
Jesus healing a deaf person (Mark 7:31-37)
Stephen being stoned (Acts 7:54-60)

Learner Goals

"Who Am I?" helps students

☆ improve non-verbal communication,

☆ expand their comfort zones in a "no right or wrong way to do it" drama,

☆ become more comfortable with their bodies,

☆ draw on previous knowledge to identify the mystery Bible person.

Preparation

Write out the names of four to ten Bible characters on individual index cards. Be familiar with the story surrounding the particular Bible person. This prepares you to call out hints if the class cannot guess and the actor needs some suggestions.

Students will be quick to come up with their own Bible characters to act out. Be ready to accept suggestions.

You will need a stopwatch or an accurate clock.

Who Am I?

 Choose one student to pick one of the mystery Bible characters. Let the student choose a familiar character or give her a card with a character on it. Give her thirty seconds or so to prepare (forty-five seconds).

 The student is given thirty seconds to act out a part of a story or activity associated with the character. The class may not guess out loud for thirty seconds (thirty seconds).

 The student continues to act out the story for another thirty seconds. But at the teacher command, "Suggestions now," the class can call out suggestions. When the character has been identified, another student can try (thirty seconds).

 The next student acts out "Who Am I?" (approximately one minute per character).

 Follow with a lively discussion after each character or at the end using the questions that follow and others you create.

Questions

○ Why is this Bible person important to us?
○ What did God ask this person to do?
○ What was this person's relationship with God?
○ If you were this person what would you have done differently?
○ Are there any people today who are like the Bible person we just watched?

Key Points

☆ Actors use no words but they can use sounds if desired. Try it both ways.
☆ Give each actor thirty seconds of acting time before the class is allowed to make a guess. This keeps the drama under control and gives the actor time to have some fun.

Extension

This drama works well with partners or small groups as well. One student from the group acts out a Bible character for the others in her group or for her partner. The actor can choose a person from the prepared cards, or pick one of her favorites.

What's the Story?

Themes and Stories

Here we have a "game-like" acting drama for the whole class. It will be so popular that, if you let them, students will act for the entire class time. In this drama one student moves to the front of the class and acts out (silently) an action from a Bible story. When the class determines the story being silently acted out, they join in the acting by doing some other activity connected with the story. Bible scenarios that have specific action are best here: fishing, building, praising, commanding, searching, and collecting. This activity is helpful to class control because the actors are silent unless you want them to make sounds or improvise dialogue. The big difference between "Who Am I?" and "What's the Story?" is that in "What's the Story?" other actors are added to the scene, making this drama more participatory.

These are a few examples of possible Bible stories:
Building the ark (Genesis 6:9-22)
Moses in the bulrushes (Exodus 2:1-10)
Samuel being called by God (1 Samuel 3:2-18)
Disciples fishing (Luke 5:1-11)
Feeding of the 5,000 (John 6:3-14)
Raising Lazarus from the dead (John 11:1-44)

Learner Goals

"What's the Story?" helps students
- ☆ identify the events and sequence of a story,
- ☆ improve non-verbal communication,
- ☆ cooperate.

Preparation

Identify stories that are filled with action. Write suggestions on index cards. These cards will be presented to the individual students who start the drama.

Have additional acting suggestions ready to call out. This will encourage students to jump in and get involved even if they cannot think of an action.

What's the Story?

 A student is picked to start the drama and is presented with a card that identifies the story. The student is given thirty seconds to plan an action from the story (one minute).

 At the front of the room the student mimes one of the actions from the story (forty-five seconds).

 After forty-five seconds classmates who think that they know the story can join in and begin acting at the front of the room. Those joining the acting must do complementary but different actions from any other actor (one minute).

 Allow as many students to join the acting as are willing. The actors can notice one another, interact, and then work together. "Freeze," stops the drama (three minutes).

 Follow each performance with lively discussion based on the questions that follow and others you create.

Questions

❍ What is important about doing your work well?
❍ Why does God give us occupations or jobs to do?
❍ How were we able to recognize what job or activity the actor was doing?
❍ How can others tell how we are feeling even though we don't tell them?

Key Points

☆ If the students are slow to join in or if they cannot guess the character, the teacher can name the story. This "jump starts" the action.
☆ Suggest some different but complementary actions out loud to get hesitant students involved.
☆ Remember that the acting is silent until the teacher says otherwise.

Extensions

When enough students are silently acting out the actions of the story say, "Freeze—no one move. When I say, 'Go,' all those up front will begin saying what they think their characters might say." Bring it to life for a short time. Encourage actors to offer suggestions when acting.

Two-Person Drama

Themes and Stories

These short Two-Person Dramas place students in dramatic opposition to one another. Bible stories are filled with conflict between two characters.

To set up this drama, the class must be placed in pairs—one person could be Moses, for example, and the other person could be Pharaoh. Each paired drama could have Moses finding reasons for Pharaoh to "let my people go." Each Pharaoh could answer with reasons why the Israelites should remain in Egypt as slaves. All pairs would do the drama simultaneously. The more your class does "Two-Person Dramas," the quicker and deeper the students drop into the roles you provide for them. How these challenges are played out give students insight into God's love for his people. What is also great about this drama is that it can be played out with very little room.

These are a few possible stories:
Moses convincing Pharaoh to let the Israelites go (Exodus 7-13)
David convincing Saul to let him fight Goliath (1 Samuel 17:28-40)
Peter trying to convince people that he didn't know Jesus (Matthew 26:69-75)
Look under "Preparation" to find more suggestions.

Learner Goals

The "Two-Person Drama" helps students
★ recognize the faithfulness of God in difficult situations,
★ become familiar with the stories as they defend their opposing positions,
★ improve concentration,
★ improve verbal skills.

Preparation

Identify a story which has two characters with opposing views. Read over the story to understand the background of the two arguments. Write out three or four arguments for each of the two characters. Here are some scenarios:

Person 1: David
Person 2: King Saul
Conflict: How can David convince a skeptical King Saul that he can defeat the giant Goliath? What has David done in the past to prove he can fight? Why does Saul give David the armor?
Scripture: 1 Samuel 17:28-40

Person 1: Pesky Neighbor
Person 2: Sleeping Friend
Conflict: The pesky neighbor begs for food at midnight. How will he convince his sleeping friend to open the door and give him what he needs? What kind of a busy day does the sleeping friend have tomorrow? He needs his sleep!
Scripture: Luke 11:5-8

Two-Person Drama

For ease of understanding, I will use Moses challenging Pharaoh as the two-person conflict. Feel free to use any story with two opposing characters.

 Read the Bible story to the class. In this example, Moses demands of Pharaoh, "Let my people go!" (two minutes).

 Divide the class into pairs in which one person is Moses and the other is Pharaoh (one minute).

 The initiator of the challenge (in this case, all of the students who are Moses) always takes three steps away from his or her partner (all of the Pharaohs). With the students' eyes closed, remind the class about the conflict. What does Pharaoh want and what are some of his arguments? What can Moses do to convince Pharaoh? (one minute).

 With eyes open, Moses begins the drama by moving to Pharaoh and challenging him. Complete the challenge, then reverse roles (two minutes).

 Follow with lively discussion based on the questions that follow and others you create.

Questions

○ What was it like to be the first character? The second character?
○ Who would you rather be? Why?
○ What did you learn about this story when you were a person in it?

Key Points

☆ If students begin laughing too much and are not concentrating on the roles, call, "Freeze!" Bring the initiating characters three steps away from their partners and have them begin again.
☆ The most critical time is the moment when you say, "Moses (or some other character), walk to Pharaoh and begin to convince him." If there is silence because no one speaks, then embarrassing laughter is sure to follow. Say, "Freeze!" and have the students close their eyes. Say, "Moses, think about the first thing you will say to Pharaoh. Now open your eyes and when I say "Go," begin the drama—Go!"
☆ This drama works in small places.

Extensions

Provide a different scene and characters for each pair. Have the pairs rehearse the scene several times. Each time the students should try to add more to the dialogue and make the argument or challenge more interesting. Ask them to make the scene two minutes in length and decide who will win in their drama. Have each pair perform the short drama for the rest of the class.

Take these "Two-Person Dramas" to other classrooms at your church. Link the various scenes together by having a narrator introduce each story briefly.

TV Personality

Themes and Stories

What would happen if the students in your class could experience five or six fascinating characters from the Bible, all within a five-minute time span? I think there would be a burst of creativity, noise, and enthusiasm. "TV Personality" opens the way for students to become whatever character the teacher calls out. Picture this—the teacher, standing at a central point so that all the students can see her, represents a television camera. Students must act out the designated Bible character and action as if they were in front of a TV camera. The teacher must always have eye contact with the students.

These are some suggested Bible characters and dramatic situations:
The snake's view of how he got Adam and Eve to eat the fruit
What it was like walking through the Red Sea
Balaam's donkey talking about how dumb Balaam was
How Gideon attacked the Midianites
David talking about how he prepared to fight Goliath
A chef making a special Christmas cake
An explorer talking about how she/he discovered Noah's ark

Pick wild situations and characters and have fun!

Learner Goals

"TV Personality" helps students
* ☆ think more quickly,
* ☆ become more animated when they speak,
* ☆ use and extend the knowledge of Bible stories that they have,
* ☆ build confidence when speaking.

Preparation

Create a list of five to ten Bible characters or imaginary characters who could be related to the Bible (an explorer looking for Noah's ark, for example), and an action for each. Try to provide ample space for the students. Decide on a central location where you can stand so students can see you, the "camera lens."

TV Personality

 The class stands so that all of the students can see the eyes of the teacher (one minute).

 Instruct the class that they will all be the same Bible character on a TV show. As the various characters are named the whole class together must instantly try to tell their story, in character, to the camera/teacher (one minute).

 Call out the first character (for example, David talking about how he prepared to fight Goliath). Give students five seconds to silently prepare and then call "Go." Students talk to the "camera" in the most dramatic way possible. Students act out the same character simultaneously and should all speak at one time. Each student must face the camera (which is the teacher). After twenty-five seconds call "Freeze!" (thirty seconds).

 Call out the rest of the characters. Call "freeze" after twenty-five seconds and then change the character (thirty seconds times number of characters).

 Follow with lively discussion based on the questions that follow and others you create.

Questions

○ What was your favorite character? Why?

○ Do you think (choose one of the characters) was like us? How?

○ What was special about this particular character? Why do you think God chose him?

○ How has television changed the way Christians spread the message of Christ?

○ What do you think the Bible will look like in the future? How will people read it?

Key Points

☆ This drama can be noisy and somewhat chaotic. That is just fine. Use the control command "Freeze!" to bring students to silence after each Bible character. I often raise my hand when I say "Freeze!" This gives a visual cue as well as a vocal one.

☆ Use a stop watch to keep the dramas short and to keep students focused.

☆ Students must keep talking and inventing as they go.

☆ Give only five seconds to prepare.

☆ The class must always face the camera.

Ace Reporter

Themes and Stories

This drama is based on a "Two-Person Drama" format (each student has a partner). One person is the reporter with questions and the other person is the Bible character to be interviewed. As the reporter interviews the Bible character, both students learn about the story and the characters associated with that story. The "Ace Reporter" fits with just about any story that has a central character in it. Also remember that you can interview "witnesses" that are not central figures. An example from the stories below would be interviewing the captain of Paul's ship.

Here are some examples:
Adam or Eve banished from Eden (Genesis 3:3-24)
Noah building the ark (Genesis 6:9-22)
Joshua and the walls of Jericho (Joshua 6)
Mary, Joseph, or a shepherd witness Jesus' birth (Luke 2)
Paul's nephew hears a plot (Acts 23:12-22)
Paul is shipwrecked (Acts 27:27-44)

Learner Goals

The "Ace Reporter" helps students
☆ get into dramatic speaking roles in a playful, non-threatening manner,
☆ practice imaging (painting pictures with their imaginations),
☆ comprehend and restate the story line of a Bible story.

Preparation

Provide a copy of the reporter questions found at the end of this drama or write them on the chalkboard so all can see. Find a story that has three or four characters in it. This story will be read to the class.

Ace Reporter

 Read the selected story (two minutes).

Divide the class into pairs in which one person is the reporter and the other is the actor. Reporters are given the questions to look at while the actor decides which of the three or four characters they wish to become. In the story of Paul being freed from prison, Paul, Silas, or the jailer are choices to act out (two minutes).

 Reporters ask the questions of the Bible characters. Actors answer the questions as the Bible character using as much description as possible (two minutes).

 Reverse roles. Encourage the actors to choose new characters. This keeps the drama fresh (three minutes).

 Follow with lively discussion based on the questions that follow and others you create.

Questions

○ In what ways is your character similar to you? How is he or she different?
○ Could you imagine where this story takes place?
○ What parts of the story did you know best?
○ What was this person's relationship to God?
○ What mistakes did the character in this story make?

Key Points

☆ Before the interview begins, have the students close their eyes. Remind the reporters and actors about the story's strongest images.
☆ Consider using an overhead projector to display the reporter's questions.
☆ You can create your own reporter questions. Choose ones that bring out feeling as well as the action in the story.

Reporter Questions

1. Tell me, in your own words, what happened. There must be more to the story—what else happened?
2. What was your part in the story—what did you do or see?
3. Describe for me how you felt as this story was happening around you. How did you feel afterward?
4. What do you think is important about this story?
5. Why do you think God allowed this to happen?

See It, Be It

Themes and Stories

This drama allows students to use their own imaginations and experiences to create a background for acting out a Bible character. To "See It," the students close their eyes and listen. Begin to describe the setting of the chosen story—the actions of the people, the sounds that might be present, the buildings, the landscape, and the environment. When you describe a tree or a wall, the students can imagine each object.

To "Be It," ask the students to see themselves in the picture as the key person in the story. When the students open their eyes they can move around the classroom pretending to be the Bible character. The whole class can become the wise men bringing a gift to Jesus, or Samson striding among his enemies. Once the students are in-role, suggest movement ideas.

Here are some examples:
A builder at the tower of Babel (Genesis 11:1-9)
Moses, hiding from the Egyptian soldiers (Exodus 2:11-15)
King Nebuchadnezzar as a beast of the field (Daniel 4:29-34)
Zacchaeus climbing the tree to see Jesus (Luke 19:1-9)
A guard at the cross of Jesus just as the darkness strikes (Matthew 27:45-54)

Learner Goals

"See It, Be It" helps students
☆ strengthen their imaginations,
☆ personalize Bible characters and environments,
☆ move creatively.

Preparation

Identify a story that has a specific or unusual character in it. Write out a description of that Bible character on an index card. If no specific information is given, then create your own (for example, John the Baptist sat by a fire, at night, the wind was blowing, locusts were his only meal, his hair was long, his clothes were made of camel hide, what did they smell like?).

Write on an index card some belief-building actions that fit with the story, such as moving through water, sneaking up on something or someone, finding shelter, etc.

Create a space for some movement (stack tables and chairs if possible).

See It, Be It

 Remove tables and chairs (if possible). Have students go to a place of their own where they have a bit of room around them. Ask them to sit and close their eyes (one minute).

 Ask the students to remember their favorite outside place. "Picture this in the TV screen of your mind." Ask questions about what they see (although no one answers out loud). Do they see and hear the trees, weather, running water, wind, animals, and build-ings? (one and a half minutes).

 Ask students to see a Bible character in their scene (John the Baptist, for example). Describe what John the Baptist looks like. Is he tall? Does he smell? Is he wearing rough clothing? (one minute).

 Say "when you open your eyes you will be John the Baptist. You will begin to prepare a campground for the night (hiding/working/preparing—depending on the action of your story). Open your eyes." Then lead the students to build the shelter by doing "belief-build-ing" activities (four minutes).

 Follow with lively discussion based on the questions that follow and others you create.

Questions

○ What was special about this Bible character?
○ What mistakes did the Bible character make in the Bible story?
○ Were you able to remember the feel of the wind or smell of something special?
○ Why is the place you remembered important to you?

Key Points

☆ When the students open their eyes and begin to move, don't let them look at each other or come into physical contact with each other. This is an individual drama.

☆ Build belief with exciting and exact actions for students— sneak, build, eat, sharpen, change clothes, etc.

☆ Movements do not need to cover distance. The students can create the drama around their personal spaces. It does not take much room to build a shelter, cook a meal, look for signs of the enemy, etc.

☆ When describing the story setting, use the five senses to help make the environment real.

Visual Art Drama

Themes and Stories

One of the seldom-noticed weaknesses of Christian education in general is the lack of evocative biblically inspired pictures—ones that lead us to dream, get excited, wish we were there. Pictures should drip with mystery and passion and wonder. Simply put, "Visual Art Drama" involves asking good emotional questions about a story-based picture (non-abstract). Then, once the story line and the dramatic struggle has been identified, the teacher leads the students into becoming one of the people in the picture. My advice is to first find a great picture and then do the drama based on the character in that picture. If you do it the other way around—look for a picture to fit a character (or theme)—you will spend many hours looking for the perfect picture. If you are excited about "Visual Art Drama" then your mission is this—go out and find these types of pictures. Look for pictures in old curriculum material, posters, and teaching aids, as well as museum prints. One way that I build a picture file is to take a color photograph of a picture that moves me. Then, if not prohibited by copyright, I make a color transparency out of it and use it on an overhead projector. Alternatively, take picture of the art to a photocopying business, and have them make can overhead transparency. However, if the picture is large enough for the entire class to see, it is simplest just to show it to them.

Learner Goals

"Visual Art Drama" helps students
★ identify and appreciate the "artistic tension" found in visual art,
★ identify the key spiritual struggle in a Bible story,
★ enter into the emotional struggle of Bible characters.

Preparation

Remove tables and stack chairs (if possible). Have some good questions prepared, such as "What is this person in the picture thinking right now?" "What is he/she doing?" "Why is this character wearing this type of clothing?" "What do you think will happen ten minutes after the story occurred?"

After students have "become" the character in the picture, have some belief-building activities ready to lead the students (for more suggestions and background on "role" and "building belief," see Story Drama 6: Teacher-Led Drama).

Visual Art Drama

 Move tables and chairs. Have students sit so they can all see the picture (two minutes).

 Ask questions of individual students based on the relationships, actions, and environment within the picture (two minutes).

 Ask students to pick one person in the picture that they like. Then ask the students to move away from the picture and take the shape of that character. Say "Eyes closed." (one minute).

 Describe the environment and the dramatic activity that their character will have to do. Say "Eyes open. Begin moving as that character." Verbally lead the students into doing picture-related actions or belief-building actions (three minutes).

 Follow with lively discussion based on the questions that follow and others you create.

Questions

○ What do think the person in the picture is doing? Why is he or she doing it?

○ What do you think this person is feeling?

○ What might he or she be saying?

○ If you could actually become one of the people in this picture, which one would you be and why?

Key Points

☆ The pictures need not be large or full-color (although both of these help). They must, however, be more than smiling patriarchs who look holy. Remember, drama is about people in a mess, and these pictures need to hint at or represent the struggle to resolve the mess.

☆ You can use slides pulled from books of pictures. These can be made with an ordinary camera. Although you should abide by copyright laws, for certain educational purposes short excerpts from books may be copied.

☆ You might also try enlarging a picture on a color photocopier.

PART 5

Theme Dramas

Drama usually exposes students experientially to the truths or themes found in a specific story. "Theme Dramas" work differently. You can first identify a biblical theme you wish to teach, and then, using one of the "Theme Dramas," choose a variety of stories to illustrate that theme. Finding ways to teach themes like forgiveness, repentance, the danger of envy, servanthood, and faith can be time consuming. "Theme Drama" is a quick way to have students actively learn a biblical theme or concept.

For instance, if you wish to teach the concept "trusting the Lord," you may choose Theme Drama 1: Blind Walk. In this drama, students are blindfolded so that they have to trust their partners to lead them around. Trust, an abstract concept, is thus physicalized in the experience.

I encourage you to use each exercise more than once, each time emphasizing a different learner goal or story. This is especially true for "Mystery Box," "Group Statues," and "Machines." I recommend that you begin with either "Blind Walk" or "Mirrors," which are both simple and sure-fire.

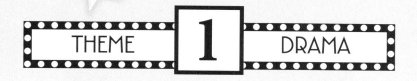

Blind Walk

Themes and Stories

This experience is a great confidence and trust builder for students. I love this simple drama because time and again, after students have walked through it, they are amazed at how helpless they felt when blindfolded. Their comfort zones are stretched. It also takes some courage for a student to place his decision-making power into the hands of another. This theme drama gives an experience basis from which to discuss topics about leadership, God's guidance, trust, and faith in God. Students revel in the new sensory experience of sound and touch (when sight is removed). This is a wonderful dramatic event to set up for your students. There can be a tremendous awakening of senses.

These are some Scriptures that talk about these themes:
Abraham's journey (Genesis 12, Hebrews 11:8-19)
Living by faith, not by sight (2 Corinthians 5:7)
Trusting in the Lord (Proverbs 3:5, 6)
Our lives belong to God (Jeremiah 10:23)

Learner Goals

"Blind Walk" helps students
☆ learn to trust others,
☆ give up control,
☆ rediscover the richness of touch, smell and sound,
☆ identify with the visually challenged.

Preparation

You will need one blindfold for every two students. I suggest that you rip old pieces of cloth to make blindfolds.

If the class has an odd number of students you will have take a partner.

Clear the room of tables (some obstacles are fine) or move to an open area.

Blind Walk

 Divide the class into pairs (everyone has a partner). Give one blindfold to each pair. One student will be sighted, the other will be blind (one minute).

 Demonstrate (using one student) how to lead the blind partner by supporting the partner's hand. Describe the area surrounding the partner while always protecting him (one minute).

 Place the blindfold on one student from each pair. Ask the other student to lead his partner slowly around the room negotiating objects on the floor and exploring the room by touch. If both you and students feel confident, the drama can be taken outside of the classroom (three minutes).

 After a few minutes have the partners switch. The sighted becomes blind and blind becomes sighted (three minutes).

 Follow with lively discussion based on the questions that follow and others you create.

Questions

○ What did you touch that felt unusual to you? Any unusual smells?

○ Describe some of your feeling during the walk.

○ Was it hard to give up control to someone else? In what ways?

○ Has God ever asked you to do something very specific? Did you know how it would turn out?

Key Points

☆ Stress the need to keep the blind partners safe. They rely totally on the sighted person. Remember also that this is a drama that is to build trust between students.

☆ Prepare the class to take the drama outside of the classroom. Set boundaries so that they know where they can lead their partners and where they must not go. Also set a time limit.

☆ I suggest that younger students remain in an enclosed environment.

Mirrors

Themes and Stories

"Mirrors" is a non-vocal drama that takes up little space. It is a real concentration booster that also builds up a student's trust and confidence in a classroom. To set up "Mirrors" the class must be placed in pairs and asked to sit facing one another. All pairs will do the drama simultaneously. One student, as leader, will move hands, face, and body in a variety of patterns. The other student will be the follower and "mirror" each and every action that the leader makes. The object is to be so "in-tune" that an observer cannot see who is the leader and who is the follower.

This drama-active event helps students understand the truth found in a variety of themes such as obedience to God and becoming like Christ. Mirrors is a great way to experience how we, as Christians, are to be mirrors of Christ. What Christ does we should do. We are also being "conformed to the likeness of his Son" (Romans 8:29). "Mirrors" is a physical way to understand the leading of the Holy Spirit and to explore what it means to follow God's commands.

These are some themes and verses to use with "Mirrors:"
Elisha patterning himself after Elijah (2 Kings 2)
Teaching others (2 Timothy 2:2)
Being an example (Titus 2:7)
Hearing and doing (James 1:22)

Learner Goals

"Mirrors" helps students
☆ gain confidence in themselves,
☆ increase concentration for sustained time periods,
☆ understand how to synchronize and cooperate with someone.

Preparation

If possible have the tables cleared so that more exploratory work can be done by students. Be ready to move around the room to encourage the pairs of students to "stay at it."

Locate some Scriptures that reflect on the theme of following.

Mirrors

 1 Divide your class into pairs in which one student is the leader and the other is the "mirror" (one minute).

 2 The pairs sit facing each other either on the floor or in chairs. At the command "Begin," the leader of the pair slowly (and I mean slowly) begins to move his or her arms (one minute).

 3 The follower mimics or mirrors the movements of the leader exactly and at the same time. It should appear as if the leader is in front of a mirror. The follower watches the leader's eyes only (two minutes).

 4 Have partners try to stand up or make facial expressions. Instruct them to do this slowly and with no delay between leader and mirror. Reverse roles (four minutes).

 5 Follow with lively discussion based on the questions that follow and others you create.

Questions

○ Why was it hard to look into each others eyes?
○ When your partner moved fast, what happened to your movement?
○ Is Jesus always on time when we need him? How do we know this?
○ How does the Bible give us signals so that we can follow Jesus?

Key points

☆ The students must move slowly or the follower will not be able to "mirror" the leader. The most important thing is for students to slow down. Speed up and this drama will not work.
☆ The drama activity can be done with two students sitting in chairs facing one another.
☆ Instruct students to look at their partners' eyes and rely on peripheral vision.

Extensions

Repeat the drama, but do not define a leader in the pairs. Let the leadership go back and forth between the two students. The object is to not indicate when the leadership changes. Students mutually decide who should lead when.

Have a contest to determine who is the best mirror pair. As the leadership transfers back and forth between the students, the teacher looks for any indication as to who is leading and who is following within each pair. If it can be determined who is leading, then the teacher touches the leader on the shoulder and that pair is out of the game. Who will be last standing pair?

One Word Circle Story

Themes and Stories

In this drama, the class can take just about any theme and create a story around it. Themes such as lost and found, being mean, can't do it right, and topics such as shyness, bullies, and freedom are all useful. The teacher tells the students that the story they are about to make up is about a girl who is really mean (for example). Each person in the circle will add one word at a time so that a story is built word by word. For example, a story about mean Elizabeth might be built like this: "It–was–a–strange–day–when –Elizabeth–woke–up–and–said–to–her–cat–I–feel–mean–today." Use the curriculum theme for the week. Then, after the class has created one or two "One Word Circle Stories," the teacher can move right on into a Bible story that illuminates the same theme.

These are some suggested stories:
The Creation (Genesis 1, 2)
Noah and the Ark (Genesis 6–8)
Joseph (Genesis 37–50)
The Battle of Jericho (Joshua 6)
David and Goliath (1 Samuel 17)
The Feeding of 5,000 (Matthew 14)

Learner Goals

"One Word Circle Story" helps students
☆ build imagination,
☆ sustain concentration for a period of time,
☆ build community,
☆ develop story continuity.

Preparation

Pick out this week's theme from the curriculum. Have a few ideas ready to begin building the story. Be able to create a circle or square (tables should be moved if possible).

One Word Circle Story

1 Form the class into a circle or square. Tables should be moved if possible although chairs can be used (one minute).

2 Begin the "One Word Circle Story" by telling the class: "This is the story about a boy (or girl) who couldn't do anything right (as an example of a theme about God accepting us just as we are). Where should we start the story?" The students will give suggestions (thirty seconds).

3 The teacher begins with the first word (for example, "It"). The student to the right of the teacher then adds the next word to build the story (for example, "was") and looks to his right. The next student adds her one word to the story and then looks to the person on the right to add the next word. Each student adds one word and continues the story (two minutes).

4 The teacher can jump in at any time to focus the group or to help them out with a word. At the end of the story, move into reading the Bible story related to the same theme (two minutes).

5 Follow with a lively discussion as you compare the Bible story with the class story.

Questions

○ How was the person in our story similar to the character in the Bible story?

○ What was the most interesting part of our story?

○ Is it hard to believe that the original Bible stories really happened? Why or why not?

Key Points

☆ Make sure that each student adds only one word.

☆ Jump in often to keep the story going.

☆ Read the looks on the students' faces. If the students seem to be struggling, provide a single word suggestion to remove undue pressure.

Extension

Try to build a Bible story using only one word at a time. Begin with a story that the class is somewhat familiar with. Each person in the circle will add one word at a time so that a story is built word by word (for example "God–said–to–Jonah–'Go–talk–to–the–people–of–Nineveh.'"). Students tend to add modern objects (such as flashlights, cars, and life boats) or change the story line a bit. As the story will not end up exactly as it is in the Bible, be sure to "debrief" (talk about where the stories are different).

Mystery Box

Themes and Stories

This drama is more of an imaginative active learning game than a drama that needs to be linked to one specific theme. It opens the door for individual students to both hold and shape imaginary objects and to choose what mystery object they will make appear from the box. The class sits in a circle. The teacher takes a number of mimed (imaginary) objects out of an invisible box. The students then guess what the objects are. The teacher gives clues to the students by defining the weight, size, essence, and use of that object. After the teacher creates several objects, each student, in turn, can try to create an object. They must create the size, weight, and use of the object. The other students guess what the object is.

The next step is to have students pull out objects from a Bible story. As each object is created, the teacher can point out the significance of that object to the particular story. The imaginary object is then passed around the circle so each student can handle it.

These are some suggested objects:
Unleavened bread as Israel leaves Egypt
The tablets of stone given to Moses
King Saul's crown
David's sling

Learner Goals

"Mystery Box" helps students
☆ use their imaginations,
☆ personalize abstract and unfamiliar objects that are important to the Christian faith,
☆ concentrate better.

Preparation

Be able to seat students in a rough circle (tables cleared). Sitting around a table can work if necessary (although not as much movement is possible).

Have a list of interesting objects and the stories that correspond to those objects.

Mystery Box

 Have the class sit in a circle. Explain that everyone has an imaginary mystery box. Demonstrate by miming (defining by hand movements) the size and shape of the box (thirty seconds).

 Open the lid and slowly pull an imaginary object from the box (for example, the lost lamb from the parable). The class observes how you handle the object—its weight, movement (is it alive?), size, bendability, etc. (one minute).

 The students guess what the object is and the Bible story that it comes from, if applicable. When the object has been identified, move on to the next object to be created, whether by you or by a student (thirty seconds).

 A student creates his or her own mystery box and pulls an imaginary object from it. As it is handled by the student others in the class guess what it is (one minute times the number of students).

 Follow with lively discussion based on the questions that follow and others you create.

Questions

○ What purpose did this object have?
○ Why was this object valuable?
○ What is unique about it?
○ What other stories might have such an object in it?

Key Points

☆ Make sure that the proper weight is assigned to the object that is being created.
☆ How an object is used (strumming a lyre, flattening and placing unleavened bread in an oven, melting down the gold for the golden calf) is the most important active clue that can be given to students.

Extension

After you create an object (for example, a snake from the Garden of Eden) it can be passed on to the student next to you. The student handles the same object for a few seconds and then passes it on down the line. Keep track of the weight and size of the object being passed. As it moves from one student to the other the transfer of weight and size should be evident. The key is to give the object the same size and feel as it passes from one to the other.

Group Statues

Themes and Stories

This is really an extension of the Character Drama 1: Statues, but with some differences. This drama is based on group work rather than a paired experience and has the potential for revealing the struggles and strengths found in human relationships.

Statues of modern scenes (using situations from school or home) can be made to elaborate the Bible stories. This is a great way to apply truths like compassion, submission, leadership, sacrifice, friendship, and the cost of betrayal.

These are some examples of Bible appropriate stories:
Adam and Eve running from the angel (Genesis 3:22-24)
Jacob, Esau, Isaac, and Rebekah during the
  betrayal of Isaac (Genesis 27)
Moses smashing the tablets of stone as Israel
  worships the golden calf (Exodus 32:19-24)
Peter, James, and John with Jesus on the
  Mount of Transfiguration (Luke 9:28-36)
Jesus and the disciples when Judas betrays
  Jesus with a kiss (Luke 22:47-53)

Learner Goals

"Group Statues" helps students
☆ concentrate for extended periods,
☆ overcome reluctance to being part of a group,
☆ begin to identify and then understand the truth behind a Bible story.

Preparation

Choose stories that have groups of people in them. Identify the moment in the story that shows the struggle or strength between this group of people, and write this out on an index card. That moment is what the statue will represent.

Have enough stories for the number of groups in your class. You will need spaces for each group to create its statue. Plan to move the tables or use another open space.

Group Statues

 Divide your class into groups in which each group contains three students or more. The groups then decide who is the sculptor and who will be the clay people (one minute, thirty seconds).

 Give each sculptor a card with a group struggle on it. The sculptor reads the card and thinks about the picture while the rest of group sits for thirty seconds (thirty seconds).

 On the command "Go!" all sculptors simultaneously shape their groups to show the struggle or success of these people taken from the Bible story. Count down so groups know when time is up (two minutes).

 Each group should recreate their sculpture for the rest of the class (two minutes times the number of people).

 Follow with lively discussion based on the questions that follow and others you create. You may wish to discuss each "Group Statue" when it is finished.

Questions

○ What would be the message of this statue for you?
○ Have you ever been in a situation similar to this?
○ What did these Bible characters do right or wrong?
○ If you were these people, what would you do?

Key Points

☆ Keep moving around and encouraging groups to concentrate.
☆ Noise should be at a minimum. Encourage this to be a silent project.
☆ Use the command "Freeze" to keep the statue focused when time is up.

Extensions

Each person within a group can create his or her own group statue. The statues will be created from a story chosen by the student. If there are four people in a group then you will ultimately have 4 four-person group statues. These can be shown to the rest of the class, or the sculptors of other groups can view each other's work.

Create a statue that illustrates a Bible story, but place the statue in a modern situation.

Machines

Themes and Stories

This drama is difficult to explain yet fairly easy to do. Each student uses sound and movement to become a component in a large, multi-level, imaginary machine.

Think of it this way. How would you use a group of six students to create an electric mixer? Students would become the beaters, the motor, the electric plug, the bowl, and the electricity.

The "electric mixer" idea is not very spiritual, but a "disciple machine" provides great images, phrases, and physical actions to use in a machine: pulling in fish, cutting the guard's ear when defending Jesus in the Garden of Gethsemane, Judas counting silver coins, filling the baskets after the miracle of the "five loaves and two fishes," and bailing out the sinking boat. Notice the different levels suggested by the various actions performed by the disciples (picking up, pulling, attacking, kneeling). The students need to choose a specific action and corresponding sound, then continually repeat it, like a machine.

These are some suggested "Machines:"
The "What Would Heaven Be Like?" Machine
The Peer Pressure Machine
The Temptation Machine
The Christmas Machine

Learner Goals

"Machines" helps students
☆ cooperate,
☆ move creatively,
☆ develop sensitivity,
☆ develop respect and courtesy for others.

Preparation

When you pick a theme, make sure to make a short list of objects, people, and actions that relate to that theme (for example the Christmas machine—wise men, eating, modern gifts, "no room at the inn," angels). Students will provide many of their own words and actions, but some students may need a suggestion from you.

A modest open space will be needed. The amount of space depends on the size of the class. Students can move from chairs to create the "Machine" in the open area.

Machines

 Form one large circle with students seated. Present the theme to the class. They are to find a character, a repetitive action, a sound, or phrase based on that theme (one minute).

 One student moves to the center and begins the repetitive action and sound/phrase. Encourage and reinforce the need to make a sound. Let the rhythm and machine movement become established before others join in (thirty seconds).

 One by one, other students move into the center and add their own individual movement and sound. Suggest that students connect or link up physically if possible (three minutes).

 Add as many students to the thematic machine as fit the machine (even the whole class). Watch for movements that cannot be sustained (deep knee bends) as this shortens the machine's life (two minutes).

 Follow with a lively discussion based on the questions that follow and others you create.

Questions

○ Describe some interesting parts of the "Machine."
○ In what ways was the message of this "Machine" made clear?
○ Who were some of the Bible characters in our "Machine?"
○ What were some of the lessons we can learn from this machine?

Key Points

☆ Students should be connected in at least one place if possible. With beginning groups, however, the first step is to get them to offer a sound, phrase, or movement.
☆ Encourage students to use different levels (standing, lying down, squatting, stretching).
☆ Re-do one of the "Machines" with you as director—adjust the student choices to be more creative and interesting.
☆ The size of the "Machine" may grow to include the whole class.
☆ Give instructions for the "Machine" to speed up, slow down, explode, etc.

Extension

Let the students make a "Machine" that is based on creativity alone—without establishing a theme. They will make movement and sound choices based solely on what the students ahead of them have made. In a discussion afterward, determine a name or theme for the "Machine."

PART 6

Performance
Suggestions

Dramatic learning that takes place within a classroom setting is exciting and valuable. However, there are also educational benefits connected with performance—that unique experience that takes place when an actor steps in front of an audience. Performance gives students an opportunity to minister to others. Students need to learn to be of service to others, and performance is one enjoyable way for them to serve.

Common Suggestions for All Performances

After the sketch has been created, rehearse with a sense of where the audience will be. This makes all of the action viewable by the audience. Use suggested costuming (scarves, hats, coats) rather than full costumes.

One effective way to begin a sketch is to place the whole group in a single file at the back of the stage. The students must look straight ahead and not move. From this position students can move quickly into the opening frozen picture of whatever sketch you are performing.

When I refer to a "narrator," you can think of one, two, or even several actors who will all trade off handling the speaking role. In the script or story, allocate each line to one of the narrators you wish to use.

Of the twenty drama-active approaches to learning found in this book, I feel those listed below are the ones that can best be shaped into a performance experience:

☆ Sound Effect Story
☆ Music Story
☆ Moving Pictures
☆ Two-Person Drama

Sound Effect Story Performance

Performance Characteristics

Think of this performance as a radio play done live in front of an audience. A narrator (or narrators) will tell the story. At each sound event in the story (for example, wind) the actors make the appropriate sound effects. Think about using a keyboard synthesizer to add certain more difficult sounds, but do not let this dominate the experience. Costumes are not necessary, but microphones are extremely helpful.

Step-by-Step

Create a script and determine who will narrate. Indicate in the script where sounds are needed.

Have the group create the sounds needed in the story. Include sounds such as wind, marching soldiers, noisy animals, slamming doors, trumpets, laughter, and screams.

Rehearse it several times. Use microphones if necessary.

Music Story Performance

Performance Characteristics

Because "Music Story" is a wordless drama, it is great for children who have trouble being heard or for cross-cultural performances. The few words spoken to introduce the story can be easily translated. Make sure the music can be heard by both the actors and the audience.

Step-by-Step

A narrator will tell the story, probably reading directly from the Bible. The narrator introduces and interprets the students' "storytelling movement" for the audience.

Have the students freeze in the starting position of the story while the narrator speaks. When the music starts, the students come to life and act out the story to the music as they have rehearsed.

Moving Pictures Performance

Performance Characteristics

"Moving Pictures" are able to cut to the heart of the action in a story. The first picture begins with action and without the normal preamble and set-up time found in most plays and sketches. There are fewer lines to memorize and rehearsal time is cut to a minimum. Use suggested costuming to enhance the performance.

Step-by-Step

Use a narrator to set up the first picture and give the audience some of the background of the characters. The narrator will also narrate between each of the remaining pictures. When the narrator is positioned to perform, the actors will move into the first frozen picture.

Following the first narration the group will come to life, say their lines, and freeze for three seconds. Look for a key phrase or action by one of the actors as a cue for everyone to freeze. The whole group must be able to hear or see this cue.

The group will then move into the second frozen picture and wait for the narrator to speak again. Repeat this for each of the four steps.

Two-Person Drama Performance

Performance Characteristics

Audiences will be delighted to see great biblical characters come to life at a moment of conflict. Because the students improvise the characters and dramatic situation, they are creating their own interpretations of Bible characters and their own view of the conflict, which creates an original and interesting drama. Ensure biblical accuracy as the students create the scene. Several "Two-Person Dramas" can be linked together by choosing a connecting theme. Use suggested costumes for this performance.

Step-by-Step

Assign each pair of students a different story (a story with two opposing characters). Each of the students should research his own character and the circumstances surrounding the conflict in the scene.

Have all of the pairs improvise and rehearse their scenes. Give feedback to each pair as they perform in order to shape the scene.

Introduce each scene with a brief description of the characters and the conflict. Remember, this is necessary to help the audience understand the context of the story and to help create continuity between stories.

Have pairs perform their conflicts!

A Final Word

I want to encourage you by saying that no matter what unspoken fears you hold, drama can be a vital part of Christian education in your Sunday school classroom. Just remember that everyone second-guesses a dramatic choice before it is chosen. Will the class think this drama is silly? Will I be able to keep control? Will I be embarrassed? Will this work? The answer lies in preparation. Be prepared. I firmly believe that teachers need to push beyond their comfort zones; to take a risk; to break out of the routine box. Have an adventure and try these dramas. Your students will love you for it.

God Bless
R. L. Ritz

For information on performances or Christian education workshops, please call (877) 449-1786 (toll free).